Pets at My House

Goldfish

Jennifer Blizin Gillis

Heinemann Library
Chicago, Illinois

Page layout by Kim Kovalick, Heinemann Library
Printed and bound in China by South China Printing Company Limited.
Photo research by Jill Birschbach

08 07 06 05 04
10 9 8 7 6 5 4 3 2 1
Library of Congress Cataloging-in-Publication Data
Gillis, Jennifer Blizin, 1950-
   Goldfish / Jennifer Blizin Gillis.
       p. cm. -- (Pets at my house)
   ISBN 1-4034-5053-6 (hardcover) -- ISBN 1-4034-6021-3 (pbk.)
   1. Goldfish--Juvenile literature. I. Title. II. Series.
   SF458.G6G565 2004
   639.3'7484--dc22
                                    2004003194
Acknowledgments
The author and publishers are grateful to the following for permission to reproduce copyright material:
Cover photograph by Micheal Simpson/Taxi/Getty Images

p. 4 Don Klumpp/The Image Bank/Getty Images; p. 5 Dave Bradford/Heinemann Library; pp. 6l, 11, 13, 14, 15, 16, 17, 18, 19, 21, back cover Greg Williams/Heinemann Library; p. 6r Dwight Kuhn; p. 7 Will and Lissa Funk/Alpine Aperture; p. 8 Hera Bell; p. 9 Michael Newman/Photo Edit; p. 10 Jim Nicholson/Alamy; p. 12 Tudor Photography/Heinemann Library; p. 20 Paul A. Zahl/National Geographic/Getty Images; p. 22 Photodisc Blue/Getty Images; p. 23 (from T-B) Greg Williams/Heinemann Library, Greg Williams/Heinemann Library, Photodisc Blue/Getty Images, Greg Williams/Heinemann Library, Greg Williams/Heinemann Library, Greg Williams/Heinemann Library, Greg Williams/Heinemann Library

Every effort has been made to contact copyright holders of any material reproduced in this book. Any omissions will be rectified in subsequent printings if notice is given to the publisher.
Special thanks to our advisory panel for their help in the preparation of this book:

Alice Bethke,
Library Consultant
Palo Alto, CA

Eileen Day,
Preschool Teacher
Chicago, IL

Kathleen Gilbert,
Second Grade Teacher
Round Rock, TX

Sandra Gilbert,
Library Media Specialist
Fiest Elementary School
Houston, TX

Jan Gobeille, Kindergarten Teacher
Garfield Elementary
Oakland, CA

Angela Leeper,
Educational Consultant
Wake Forest, NC

Contents

Some words are shown in bold, **like this.**
You can find them in the picture glossary on page 23.

What Kind of Pet Are These?

Pets are animals that live with people.

Some pets are soft and furry.

My pets are small and slippery.

Can you guess what kind of pets they are?

What Are Goldfish?

Goldfish are a kind of fish called **carp**.

There are standard and fancy goldfish.

6

There are big and little goldfish.

Some big goldfish live outside in garden ponds.

Where Did My Goldfish Come From?

Female fish lay eggs on plants in an **aquarium**.

The eggs are picked up with a **net**.

Tiny, pale **fry** come out of the eggs.

When they are about fifteen days old, they can become pets.

How Big Are My Goldfish?

A **fry** is about as long as the end of your finger.

In ten days, it grows to be as long as your whole finger!

My goldfish are grown-up.

They are about as big as a large coin.

Where Do My Goldfish Live?

aquarium

gravel

My goldfish live in an **aquarium**.

There is **gravel** in the bottom to keep the aquarium clean.

I put plants in the aquarium.

This gives my fish a place to hide.

What Do My Goldfish Eat?

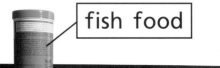

fish food

Goldfish eat special fish food.

They only eat a tiny bit at one time.

I sprinkle the food on top of the water.

The goldfish come right away!

What Else Do My Goldfish Need?

filter

Goldfish need clean water.

This **filter** helps keep the **aquarium** water clean.

airpump

Fish need lots of air to breathe.

This **airpump** puts bubbles of air into the aquarium.

What Can I Do for My Goldfish?

vacuum

I can clean the **aquarium** everyday.

This special **vacuum** cleans up dirt and food.

I change the water every week.

I wash the aquarium and put clean water in.

How Are My Goldfish Special?

Goldfish can be many colors.

They can have spots or shiny patches.

When goldfish sleep, their color is not as bright.

When they wake up, their color comes back.

Goldfish Map

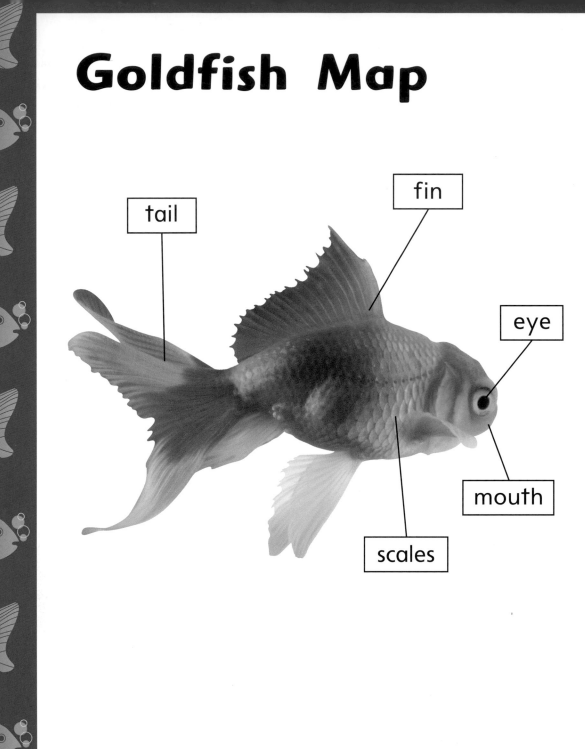

tail

fin

eye

mouth

scales

Picture Glossary

air pump
page 17
a machine that puts air into the water in
an aquarium

aquarium
pages 8, 12, 13, 16, 18, 19
kind of box with glass sides where turtles, fish,
or other pets can live

filter
page 16
machine that pulls in dirt from an aquarium and
traps it in a special cloth

fry
pages 9, 10
young fish

gravel
page 12
small pieces of rock

net
page 8
cloth with tiny holes in it that lets water go
through but keeps fish inside

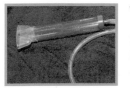

vacuum
page 18
machine that can pull in dirt and left-over food
from the bottom of an aquarium

Note to Parents and Teachers

Reading for information is an important part of a child's literacy development. Learning begins with a question about something. Help children think of themselves as investigators and researchers by encouraging their questions about the world around them. Each chapter in this book begins with a question. Read the question together. Look at the pictures. Talk about what you think the answer might be. Then read the text to find out if your predictions were correct. Think of other questions you could ask about the topic, and discuss where you might find the answers. Assist children in using the picture glossary and the index to practice new vocabulary and research skills.

❗ CAUTION: Remind children to be careful when handling animals. Pets may scratch or bite if startled. Children should wash their hands with soap and water after they touch any animal.

Index